StoRmy SeAs

STORIES OF YOUNG BOAT REFUGEES

MARY BETH LeatherDale
and ELEANOR SHAKESPEARE

annick press
toronto • berkeley

To Madzia and Shia, who taught me what it is to be in the crosshairs of history — Mary Beth
To my grandfathers, whose lives served as great examples of compassion and justice — Eleanor

© 2017 Mary Beth Leatherdale (text)
Illustrated and designed by Eleanor Shakespeare
Second printing, September 2017

Annick Press Ltd.

We acknowledge the support of the Canada Council for the Arts, the Ontario Arts
Council, and the participation of the Government of Canada/la participation du
gouvernement du Canada for our publishing activities.

Canadä

ONTARIO ARTS COUNCIL
CONSEIL DES ARTS DE L'ONTARIO
an Ontario government agency
un organisme du gouvernement de l'Ontario

Cataloging in Publication

Leatherdale, Mary Beth, author
        Stormy seas : stories of young boat refugees / Mary Beth Leatherdale ;
Eleanor
Shakespeare, illustrator.

Includes bibliographical references.
Issued in print and electronic formats.
ISBN 978-1-55451-896-8 (hardback).--ISBN 978-1-55451-895-1 (paperback).--
ISBN 978-1-55451-897-5 (epub).--ISBN 978-1-55451-898-2 (pdf)

        1. Refugees--Juvenile literature. 2. Refugee children--Juvenile literature.
3. Refugees--Anecdotes--Juvenile literature. 4. Refugee children--Anecdotes--
Juvenile literature. I. Shakespeare, Eleanor, illustrator II. Title.
HV640.L355 2017   j305.9'06914   C2016-905509-4
                                                    C2016-905510-8
Published in the U.S.A. by Annick Press (U.S.) Ltd.
Distributed in Canada by University of Toronto Press.
Distributed in the U.S.A. by Publishers Group West.

Printed in China
www.annickpress.com
www.marybethleatherdale.com
www.eleanorshakespeare.com

Also available in e-book format. Please visit www.annickpress.com/ebooks.html
for more details. Or scan

CONTENTS

INTRODUCTION

If you're reading this, you—like me—have probably won the lottery. Not the giant-check, instant-millionaire kind of lottery. The other lottery win—the really valuable one. That random, lucky break that means you were born in or immigrated to a relatively peaceful and prosperous place in the world. Along with all the other amazing things about you, that makes you pretty extraordinary.

Sixty-five million of the world's seven billion people aren't so lucky. They have been forced to leave their homes because of war, persecution, or natural disasters. Nineteen million of these displaced people have no hope of ever returning home safely and are seeking asylum in another country. More than half of these refugees are children and teenagers; many are orphans or "unaccompanied minors" traveling alone.

News reports in 2015 and 2016 have been full of stories of Syrian refugees who are risking their lives to cross the Mediterranean Sea. The civil war that has been raging there for years has forced more than half of the country's population to flee. That's more than 11 million people in need of shelter, food, water, and medical care. And thousands of others, escaping wars, persecution, and drought in the Middle East and in North and sub-Saharan Africa, are also trying to find refuge in Europe.

The influx of refugees has caused divisions across the European Union. Countless individuals and organizations have rallied to provide support to the refugees, and countries such as Germany, Hungary, and Sweden have welcomed thousands of asylum seekers. Yet many countries in Europe and North America are hostile to refugees and migrants. Anti-refugee and anti-immigrant policies are increasing around the world, depriving refugees of the right to asylum guaranteed under international law. And, hundreds of thousands of refugees are forced to pay criminal smugglers for passage across the Mediterranean on overcrowded, unseaworthy boats.

But boat refugees risking their lives at sea isn't a new phenomenon. For centuries, due to wars, famines, failing economies, and religious persecution, people have been leaving behind all they know and boarding ships for countries they've never seen. To help make sense of what I was seeing on the news, I set out to research and interview people who as children were boat refugees. I quickly understood the magnitude of what I was asking and how traumatic it can be for people to tell their stories, particularly Syrian children who have recently crossed the Mediterranean and are still living under precarious circumstances in refugee camps in Europe. The five young boat refugees whose stories appear in this book are lucky—not only did they survive the treacherous ocean voyage, but they also persevered and prospered, even in the face of uncertainty, financial challenges, and discrimination. Things got better.

At first glance, the refugees we see on the news and the hardships they endure may seem unrelated to us—not our problem. But either through action or inaction, we all play a role in the dire circumstances refugees face. For Ruth, Phu, José, Najeeba, and Mohamed, the conflicts, discrimination, and environmental challenges that forced them to leave their homes aren't their fault or within their power to change. Their courage in leaving behind everything they know in search of peace and security, and their resilience in overcoming horrific journeys, restores hope in what life can be—not just for them but for all of us.

Mary Beth

THEY CAME BY BOAT: A BRIEF HISTORY

For hundreds of years, wars, famines, failing economies, and religious persecution have forced people to leave their family, friends, and all they know behind in hope of a better life. Here are just some of the people who boarded boats seeking asylum before our stories begin.

1670

Huguenots leave France for England seeking refuge from religious persecution

1677

Mennonites sail to Pennsylvania to escape religious persecution in Germany and Switzerland

1763

Filipino sailors forced into service in their Spanish-ruled homeland jump ship and find refuge in Louisiana

1770

Facing religious and political oppression, thousands of Roman Catholics leave Ireland for North America

1809

Refugees from Saint Domingue escape fighting in the Caribbean French colony to seek asylum in New Orleans

1830
Jews leave Germany and Austria-Hungary to escape anti-Semitism

1845
Irish Potato Famine will force millions of starving Irish Catholics to immigrate to North America

1865
Crop failures force Norwegians to immigrate to North America

1868
Swedes immigrate to North America mainly due to famine

1850
Danes who converted to Mormonism immigrate to United States for the freedom to practice their religion

1914
Sikh passengers on the *Komagata Maru* arrive in British Columbia, Canada, in search of jobs. They are denied entry and forced to sail back to India, where World War I has started. Although they are British citizens, the British government distrusts them and kills 19 passengers and imprisons many others

TuRNed Away

RuTH

-----

18 YEARS OLD
BRESLAU, GERMANY
1939

> **If we go back to Germany, we will be taken off the ship into a camp and killed. People are dying in the camps—they are beaten, they are shot. We know it is a death sentence to go back.**

At last, Ruth was free.

She breathed a sigh of relief as she walked up the gangplank of the SS *St. Louis*. After trying to get out of Germany for two years, her family had finally secured passage on a ship headed to Havana, Cuba. With Hitler in power, Ruth's Jewish family had no choice but to leave. For six years, the Nazi party's anti-Semitic policies had made their life more and more difficult. Ruth's father was no longer allowed to practice law, the apartments they owned were taken away, and Ruth and her sister Margaret couldn't go to school anymore with their non-Jewish friends. In the last year, things got even worse. The Nazis incited non-Jewish Germans to take action against Jews. In a series of violent attacks known as *Kristallnacht*, Nazis and their supporters destroyed Jewish property; beat, arrested, and killed German, Czech, and Austrian Jews; and stole their valuables. To get out of Germany, Ruth's family had to turn over almost everything they owned to the Nazis. But it was worth it.

As Ruth handed over her Cuban transit visa to the ship's officer, she smiled. She was eighteen. She was crossing the Atlantic on a beautiful, luxury liner. Soon she would be swimming in the ship's pool, watching movies in the cinema, and dancing in the ballroom. She had no idea that across the Atlantic in Cuba, protesters were demonstrating to stop the 936 German Jews on the *St. Louis* from entering the country.

REPUBLICA DE CUBA
DEPARTAMENTO DE INMIGRACION
TARJETA DE IDENTIFICACION DEL PASAJERO TRANSEUNTE
IDENTIFICATION CARD OF THE PASSENGER INTRANSIT

re del pasajero   Fella Flamberg
of passenger
nalidad   sin   Nombre del Vapor   "St. Louis"
ality   Name of Steamer
fiesto No.   19   Partida No.   25
No.   Line No.
o de procedencia del pasajero   Hamburg

ANTI-SEMITISM:
HATRED OF JEWISH PEOPLE;
HOSTILITY TOWARD OR
DISCRIMINATION TOWARD JEWS

GERMANY

CUBA

The Nazi Party with Adolf Hitler as its leader came to power in Germany in 1933. The country had been through an economic depression and the Nazis used citizens' frustrations to promote their racist agenda. The Nazis said that if they rid the country of Jews and other minority groups, the "Aryan master race" would prosper. By 1945, six million Jews and hundreds of thousands of other minorities were murdered by the Nazis and their collaborators.

'Be calm.' What do they mean? Being on the *St. Louis* is like turning back time. Life is like it used to be before Hitler. Everyone is happy. We're safe in the Cuban harbor now. On Monday, we'll land and my new life will begin. Some of the passengers have a husband or a parent who is already in Cuba. All weekend long, they've been paddling out in little boats and cruising around the *St. Louis*. They holler up. We holler down. Why do they say, 'Be calm, you'll get down'? Do they think we'll fall off the gangplank?

It's been six days and the Cubans still won't let us off the boat. People are whispering that they're going to send us back to Germany. I'm so afraid. Today, I was sitting on deck talking with a friend when a man I know from Breslau came running out of the bathroom, his wrists dripping with blood, and threw himself overboard into the harbor. A sailor jumped in to save him. But the man didn't want to be saved. When he was back on deck, the man was trying to pull his arteries out. He was in the concentration camp and would rather die than go back to Germany.

DENIED

"People are WHISPERING that they are going to SEND us BACK to GERMANY."

Before the *St. Louis* even sailed from Germany, Cubans were protesting against giving the German Jews refuge. Like Germany, Cuba had recently faced an economic depression. Many Cubans resented the large number of refugees, including two thousand five hundred Jews, who had already come to the country. The Cuban newspapers, with the Nazis' help, fueled anti-immigrant and anti-Semitic sentiments, calling on the government to stop the Jewish refugees from entering the country. When the *St. Louis* arrived in the Havana harbor, the Cuban government refused to honor the Jewish refugees' transit visas and admit them into the country.

" I am not particularly INTERESTED in going to AMERICA. I am interested in STAYING ALIVE. "

"

People are screaming. Shouting. Today, they forced us to leave the Havana harbor. All day we were sitting in the ocean off the Cuban coast. Now in the middle of the night, the ship is running full steam ahead. Did we turn around? Are we back in Europe already? I jump out of bed and follow the other passengers to the captain's quarters. He explains that Jewish organizations are negotiating with other places to take us. The captain is sailing to a spot where we'll be closer if they say yes. People are worried. Frightened. The captain asks half a dozen men, including my father, to form a committee to be a liaison between the passengers and him. Telegrams arrive from the people working to save us saying, 'Don't worry, you'll get off. You will not have to go back to Germany.' Of course, nobody believes that anymore.

As we cruise along the coast, I see the lights of Miami. The palm trees look so pretty. I pray that we can land there. When we get close to shore, the US Coast Guard comes with guns. My prayers aren't working. We leave.

People want to jump overboard. If they can swim for two hours, they can make it to shore. They would rather drown than go back to Germany. If we return, we'll be taken to a concentration camp. Being sent back is a death sentence. I am not particularly interested in going to America. I am interested in staying alive. "

VOYAGE OF THE SS ST. LOUIS, 1939

MAY 13
Sails from Hamburg, Germany

MAY 27
Arrives in Havana harbor

JUNE 2
Ordered out of Cuban waters

JUNE 6
Sails back to Europe

SEPTEMBER 1
Germany invades Poland, starting World War II in Europe

ENGLAND

CUBA

"YOU'RE JUST LIVING **FROM MINUTE** TO MINUTE. YOU DO WHAT YOU HAVE TO DO. **THE** *enormity* OF IT DOESN'T HIT YOU UNTIL AFTER. THEN YOU *collapse* WHEN YOU REALIZE HOW CLOSE **YOU WERE TO** *catastrophe.*"

WHAT HAPPENED TO RUTH?

The *St. Louis* sailed back to Europe eleven days after it arrived in the Havana harbor. Jewish organizations had been furiously negotiating with Great Britain, Netherlands, Belgium, and France to allow the passengers entry. Ruth's family was sent to London, England. A few months later, after World War II started, Ruth's father managed to get passage to the United States. Ruth and her sister got jobs in New York City making gloves for the US Army and Navy. Later, Ruth went to business school and worked in an office.

Cuba was not the only country to refuse the *St. Louis* passengers entry. Argentina, Uruguay, Paraguay, and Panama were approached but also refused. After *Kristallnacht*, the United States and other countries had condemned Germany for its treatment of Jews. But when the *St. Louis* Passengers Committee cabled President Roosevelt asking for refuge in the United States, he never responded. Influential Canadians sent a telegram to Prime Minister Mackenzie King begging that he show "true Christian charity" and offer the *St. Louis* passengers sanctuary in Canada, but the government refused. At that time, Jewish people faced discrimination in the United States and Canada. Many Americans and Canadians were anti-Semitic and didn't want the government to allow Jews into the country because they thought they would steal their money and jobs. The Nazi Party drew media attention to the other countries that didn't want to admit Jewish refugees, using these incidents to defend their own persecution of the Jews.

OF THE 937 PASSENGERS ABOARD THE SS *ST. LOUIS*:

- 28 allowed to disembark in Cuba
- 1 died of natural causes en route
- 1 attempted suicide
- 288 given asylum in Great Britain
- 224 given asylum in France
- 214 given asylum in Belgium
- 181 given asylum in Netherlands
- 254 were killed in the Holocaust after returning to Europe

FIGHTing to SuRViVe

PHU

----

14 YEARS OLD
SAIGON, VIETNAM
1979

"I am sad to leave my family and afraid of being alone. At the same time, I am excited about the journey ahead. My mom says that America is a land of opportunity. "

SAIGON,
VIETNAM

↙ PULAU BIDONG
REFUGEE CAMP,
MALAYSIA

PEOPLE SMUGGLER:
A PERSON WHO FOR MONEY
ARRANGES THE ILLEGAL ENTRY
OF PEOPLE TO A COUNTRY
WHERE THEY ARE NOT
CITIZENS; PEOPLE SMUGGLING
IS A CRIME

The Vietnam War was
fought between North
Vietnam and South
Vietnam from 1955 to
1975. North Vietnam
was supported by the
Soviet Union, China,
and other communist
allies. South Vietnam
was supported by
the United States,
Philippines, and
other anticommunist
countries. When the
Americans pulled out of
the conflict in 1975, the
North Vietnamese Army
captured Saigon, in
South Vietnam, ending
the war.

UNITED STATES

"Phu, you've got to escape"

Phu stared at his mother. He couldn't believe he'd heard her correctly. Under the Communist government, it was illegal to leave Vietnam. Four years ago, when the Vietnam War ended and the North Vietnamese Army tanks came rolling into Saigon, Phu's life had changed completely. The streets he and his friends used to play on were deserted. Homes were looted. Neighbors, friends, and relatives flooded out of the city. Food was rationed and there was never enough to eat. When Phu wasn't at school, he and his little brother had to earn money for the family by walking from market to market, selling fans and traditional Vietnamese hats.

Now that Phu was fourteen, things were even worse. Vietnam had invaded Cambodia and was at war with China. Phu could soon be forced to join the army. His father and uncle had been soldiers in the South Vietnamese Army and had been killed in the war against North Vietnam. His mother didn't want him to die fighting a war. She didn't have enough money to get the whole family out of Vietnam, so she paid a smuggler $3,500—all the money she could scrape together—to buy Phu a fake passport and a space on a boat.

Phu couldn't believe he'd be leaving his family and sailing off on the South China Sea. He didn't know where the boat was going or what might happen on the way. All he knew was that escaping from Vietnam meant he had a chance of making it to the United States.

"I'm surrounded by water but I have none to drink. We've only been at sea for a few hours and already men are fighting. Hundreds of us are crammed on the boat. People are screaming and crying. I have to look after myself. There's no one here to take care of me. I have to try to make friends. I have to find some food. I have to fight to survive.

Psshew! Psshew! Psshew! Ratatatat ratatat! Pirates have boarded our boat! They point their M16 rifles into the air and fire. I cover my head and cower on deck. I hear them stomping around, threatening people until they throw the gold and dollars they have hidden into buckets. It's not the first time we've been under attack. Until now, I've been able to hide the gold ring my mother gave me. But this time it's too dangerous. I give it to them. They steal the little food and water we have, too. They force some girls my age onto their boat. What will happen to them?"

PIRATES:

PEOPLE WHO ATTACK, ROB, AND COMMIT OTHER VIOLENT CRIMES AT SEA; PIRACY IS A CRIME

"I have to FIGHT to SURVIVE."

After the Vietnam War ended, the North Vietnamese Communist government took over the South. Many South Vietnamese fled the country by air, land, or sea. The people who risked their lives on the South China Sea were called the "boat people." Three years later, the new government forced 745,000 ethnic Chinese to leave the country on overcrowded boats and the boat people became an international crisis.

As the number of Vietnamese boat people grew, Malaysia and Thailand began to refuse entry to the refugees. The United Nations called for the international community to help, brokering an agreement in which Malaysia and Thailand would let refugees come ashore if other countries like the United States and Canada agreed to resettle people within 90 days.

"Through the dark night, I can see the shore of Malaysia. 'Destroy the engine!' someone shouts. Some men smash it quickly, so they can't send us back out to sea. When we get close to shore, we hurtle ourselves off the boat, running like it's the Normandy Invasion. Some Malaysian cops see us and come towards us brandishing their batons. I haven't eaten much for the fourteen days we've been at sea and I am very weak. But when they strike me, I race back to the boat and climb aboard quickly to avoid their blows.

In the morning, the cops come back and take us to the Pulau Bidong Refugee Camp. It is very crowded—43,000 people in an area the size of three football fields—and very chaotic. I am always looking for a familiar face—a family member or an old friend from Saigon. I don't have enough food. I don't have enough water. But a couple of guys are by themselves like me. We become good friends. They are strong, and they help me. We swim in the ocean every day. We go fishing. We go up in the mountains trying to find vegetables. And we search for wood so we can cook. In a refugee camp, you have everything: fighting, friendships. You see both the good side and the bad side of people."

"IF THIS NATION WAS WILLING TO COMMIT BILLIONS OF DOLLARS AND **55,000** YOUNG AMERICANS [TO THE VIETNAM WAR] IT SHOULD BE WILLING NOW TO OFFER ITS PRECIOUS SOIL AS SANCTUARY TO THOSE WHO ARE LEFT BEHIND."

—*THE WICHITA EAGLE*

PHU'S JOURNEY

425 people on the boat

14 days at sea

17 pirate attacks

8 months in the Pulau Bidong Refugee Camp

WHAT HAPPENED TO PHU?

After eight months in the Pulau Bidong Refugee Camp, fourteen-year-old Phu flew to San Francisco. Since he was a minor (a child under eighteen), and alone, he was quickly sent to live with his cousin in "Little Saigon" in Orange County, California. Two years later, his mother, brothers, and sister escaped from Vietnam to Malaysia by boat and immigrated to California through a family sponsorship program. Phu worked to help support the family, getting a part-time job at McDonald's, cleaning toilets, working at theaters, and playing in a band. Phu hung out with other minors who had escaped from Vietnam. Since they had no family in America, Phu's mother invited them to come live with them. Phu shared his room with eight guys.

Phu and his friends faced a lot of prejudice. There were only thirty or forty Asians in his high school of more than four thousand students. People taunted him with racial slurs and Phu got into a lot of fights with the Caucasian students. Even the Vietnamese students who had come to America in 1975 and spoke better English berated the new Vietnamese students and called them FOB, "Fresh Off the Boat."

After high school, Phu enrolled in an aerospace program at California State University. He became very interested in reading about the Vietnam War and decided to join the US military. From there, he studied management and then went back to school to become a criminal defense lawyer. To pay his dues to the United States, he became a US Army Reserve Officer .

CALIFORNIA

AFTER THE VIETNAM WAR

2 million
Vietnamese left Vietnam

137,000
immigrated to Australia

500,000
died at sea

96,000
immigrated to France

823,000
immigrated to the United States

20,000
immigrated to the United Kingdom

137,000
immigrated to Canada

"MY army captain told me not to change my NAME. He said BE PROUD of your HERITAGE, because if you're not PROUD and you don't KNOW WHO YOU ARE you will not be a GOOD AMERICAN."

Stormy Seas

José

13 YEARS OLD
SANCTI SPÍRITUS, CUBA
1980

"For the first time in my life, I feel that death is a real possibility."

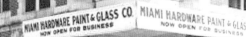

Fidel Castro led a revolt against the Cuban government called the Cuban Revolution. In 1959, Castro became the country's leader, replacing the government with a socialist state. Until that time, Cuba and the United States had a very close economic relationship. In 1961, the United States ended their diplomatic relationship with Cuba, stopping all trade and restricting travel between the countries. Castro strengthened ties with the Soviet Union and declared himself a communist.

KEY WEST, FLORIDA

HAVANA

PORT OF MARIEL

SANCTI SPÍRITUS

ASYLUM:
OFFERING PROTECTION TO THE PERSECUTED

"José, if you want to get off this boat

you can stay in Cuba." José froze as the Cuban officer walked away from the *Dulce II*. The small, two-story recreation boat was filled with thirty people—more than twice its capacity—and the captain was worried that it would not be safe to sail. Of the thousands of boats crowded into Port of Mariel harbor, this was the one an officer had ordered José and his family to board. José wasn't moving.

For decades, José's parents had wanted to leave Cuba; they didn't support the country's Communist leader, Fidel Castro, and were tired of the government controlling the food, clothing, and other goods they could buy. José's father, and thousands of other Cubans suspected of working with the United States to overthrow the government, were arrested and taken to a detention center. Almost twenty years later, they were still seen as suspicious outsiders by the government.

Since 1961, when the United States and Cuba had broken diplomatic ties, it had been almost impossible to get a visa to leave. That changed six weeks ago, after more than ten thousand people crowded onto the Peruvian embassy grounds seeking asylum. To avoid further unrest and embarrassment about Cubans' dissatisfaction with his system, Castro said anyone who wanted to immigrate to the United States could, as long as there was a boat in the Port of Mariel to take them.

Now thirteen-year-old José, his father, mother, and little sister, Leticia, were on a boat to the United States and that's where they were staying. All that stood between José and the life he dreamed of was a seven-hour boat trip. But stormy seas were ahead.

Will we ever leave Cuba? We're stuck in Port of Mariel. A big
thunderstorm hit the Gulf and it's not safe for us to sail. Even worse,
the guards order us not to leave the boat. I am so bored. All day long,
we sit huddled together on the deck in the hot, bright sun. People
are getting desperate. We're hungry. The only thing to eat is the cold
scrambled eggs and rice that the guards bring. Each day, there's even
less of that. Kids are getting sick from the heat and hunger. My mother
says I need to eat and gives me her eggs. But the smell of sweat and
vomit on the boat is so disgusting, I can barely swallow.

When we finally set sail for Florida, the sea is completely calm. An
hour into our journey, the joy on my father's face turns to concern. The
engine has died! As the captain tries to restart the motor, the calm sea
turns choppy. In a flash, high waves surround the boat. The water is
pouring in … Everyone grabs whatever they can find to bail it out. It's
no use. The water is already up to my ankles. All around me people are
screaming 'I don't want to die!'

"He... who has no REVOLUTIONARY blood, he who does not have a MIND that adapts to the IDEA of a REVOLUTION, ... We do not WANT them; we do not NEED them."

CUBAN PRESIDENT FIDEL CASTRO

"Ours is a country of REFUGEES... We'll continue to PROVIDE an OPEN HEART and OPEN ARMS to refugees seeking FREEDOM from Communist domination and from the ECONOMIC DEPRIVATION brought about by FIDEL CASTRO and his government."

US PRESIDENT JIMMY CARTER

"We're saved! A shrimp boat pulls up beside us and we pile onto it, leaving behind the few belongings we still have. The boat is already crowded with two hundred dirty, scruffy-looking men. We avoid their eyes and try to find a place to sit. When I turn around, I see the *Dulce II* sink into the sea.

A wall of water hits. Huge gusts of wind rip across the deck. We're in the tail of a storm. Waves taller than a house rock the boat. When one hits, the captain yells at us to slide to the other side to keep the boat from capsizing. Back and forth we go. One minute, it feels like we are on the top of a mountain and the next it's like we're crashing down the cliff. When night comes, it gets worse. It's impossible to sleep. Everyone is crammed together on the cold, wet, metal floor. People are so hungry and dehydrated it's like being surrounded by the dead. Everyone is just urinating and vomiting right there. The smell is overwhelming. Although I haven't gone to church in years, I begin to pray. Hour after hour after hour, I stare at the horizon looking for land. It feels like we are the only boat in the ocean."

THE MARIEL BOATLIFT, 1980

APRIL 1
Cubans drive bus into Peruvian Embassy

APRIL 4
Castro withdraws guards from the Embassy

APRIL 6
10,000 Cubans crowd into the Embassy seeking asylum

APRIL 20
Castro announces Cubans free to immigrate to United States

APRIL 21
Boats start picking up refugees

OCTOBER 31
Cuba and the United States agree to end the boatlift

"One minute, it feels like we are on the TOP of a MOUNTAIN and the next it's like we're CRASHING down the CLIFF."

WHAT HAPPENED TO JOSÉ?

After eighteen hours at sea, José's boat was rescued by the US Coast Guard and towed into Key West, Florida. José 's sister was severely dehydrated and needed medical treatment, but recovered quickly. After a few days in Miami Beach, José and his family moved to New York City, where his grandmother lived. José was shocked by the poverty and drugs in their US neighborhood and questioned why they'd left Cuba at all. He worked hard to learn English and to do well in school. After a couple of years, the family moved to the suburbs of New Jersey. For José it was like moving to another country again. He had a hard time fitting in but focused on his studies and got accepted to college. He worked at a supermarket and saved up for graduate school. Today, José is an associate professor at Florida Southern College. He returned to Cuba for the first time in 2010 to make a documentary about the Mariel Boatlift called *Voices from Mariel*.

Cuban refugees like José faced a great deal of prejudice. They were known as the "Marielitos." President Fidel Castro called the refugees *scoria* ("trash"), saying he used the Mariel Boatlift to deport Cuba's criminals and mental patients to the United States. Only about 10 percent of the people who came to the United States had a criminal record or mental health issues. Still, Americans were afraid that Cubans were untrustworthy and would take jobs from US citizens. In fact, the influx of Cuban refugees did not drive down wages or raise unemployment among Miami residents—it actually brought more jobs and businesses to the area. In 2015, Cuba and the United States restored diplomatic relationships. Travel rules have been loosened to allow Americans to travel to Cuba, but US trade to Cuba is still restricted, hurting the Cuban economy.

"When we got to the UNITED STATES I felt like I was in a MOVIE. All the colors were so much BRIGHTER, the grass greener. It was SURREAL. I couldn't believe we had SURVIVED."

CUBAN REFUGEES, 1980

- 125,000 Cubans transported to the United States
- 1,700 boats
- $1,000-per-person fee
- 90 miles (145 kilometers) from Cuba to the United States
- 27 Cubans died at sea

FeNCeD IN

NaJEEBa

II YEARS OLD
BAMIYAN, AFGHANISTAN
2000

" We are at risk of drowning on the Pacific but we prefer that risk to that of a brutal killing at the hands of the Taliban. **"**

BAMIYAN, AFGHANISTAN

PAKISTAN

INDONESIA

AUSTRALIA

A boat to Australia?

Najeeba had never been on a boat. She had never heard of Australia. The eleven-year-old didn't even know where the Pacific Ocean was. In Afghanistan, the Taliban didn't allow girls to go to school.

For Najeeba's whole life, Afghanistan had been at war. In the chaos of the fighting, the Taliban, an extremist Islamic group, rose to power. They took over Najeeba's village in Bamiyan Province. All day long she heard guns and bombs outside her mud-brick home. As members of the Hazara minority, Najeeba's family was at great risk of being persecuted and killed. With no hope of surviving, her family was forced to leave their country.

Escaping from Afghanistan was very dangerous. The Taliban were everywhere. If they saw Hazaras leaving, they would kill them. Najeeba's family sold all of their land and possessions and had enough money to pay a people smuggler to get them to Pakistan. As Hazara they were still at risk in Pakistan, so Najeeba's father found another smuggler, paying all the money they had left—$35,000—to arrange to transport the family to Australia.

After flying to Jakarta, Indonesia, Najeeba, her father, her mother, her sisters Nooria and Raihana, and her brothers Mohammed and Madhi hid in a hotel room until the boat arrived. Najeeba waited and wondered about what her life would be like in this strange new land. And then the call came: the boat was here.

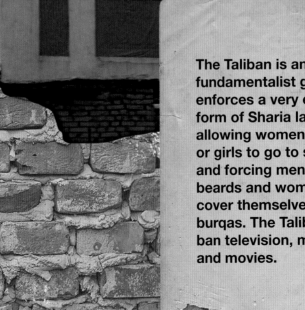

The Taliban is an Islamic fundamentalist group. It enforces a very extreme form of Sharia law, not allowing women to work or girls to go to school, and forcing men to grow beards and women to cover themselves in burqas. The Taliban also ban television, music, and movies.

"The boat is so small. I thought it would be huge like the *Titanic* but it's just a little, flimsy fishing boat. We are the last family to get on. Hundreds of adults and children are already squashed in. My mom needs to lie down but she can't even find a place to sit with the baby. Everyone else on the boat is Hazara, too. No one wants to help us, though. We cram ourselves onto the open deck, knees squashed against our chests. All I can feel around us is hostility.

I've never been on a boat before. I don't know how to swim and there are no life jackets. The smuggler said that this small boat was going to take us to meet a bigger ship. He lied. After days at sea, we are still stuck, huddled on this tiny boat. Our destiny, our future depends on this piece of wood. All I do is eat dry noodles and get seasick. That, and worry about drowning. When a thunderstorm hits and rocks the boat, we cry and hug each other goodbye."

Hazaras make up 20 percent of Afghanistan's population. They are a Shiite Muslim minority in a Sunni Muslim country. For centuries, they have been discriminated against because of the way they look and how they worship.

"Our DESTINY, our FUTURE depends on this piece of WOOD."

"Everyone makes a pact to get to AUSTRALIA or DIE."

"A hole burst in the ship during the storm! We're taking on water quickly! Sailors on an Australian Navy ship will repair the damage on one condition—that we do not go to Australia. We've already been at sea for ten days, but of course, we say yes. What choice do we have? Either they repair our boat and we give up on going to Australia, or it sinks and we drown. Once the repair is finished, they watch us until we do a U-turn and sail back toward Indonesia.

But we can't go back to Afghanistan. There is no hope for us there. Everyone makes a pact to get to Australia or die. Another U-turn and we're heading back to Australian waters. When we get close, the Navy comes out to stop us. But we don't stop. We scream and beg them to let us in. We keep going. Now they have to give us asylum."

Captains and crews are obligated under international maritime law to help vessels in danger. And, under international law, a refugee must not be forcibly returned to a country where his or her life or freedom would be endangered. Once a refugee or asylum seeker has come onto a nation's territory—including its territorial waters—the country is obligated to help the person seeking asylum.

"We made a mistake. We came to Australia to find a safe home but I think we have been captured by a different kind of Taliban—with blue eyes, blond hair, and big guns. They've taken us to the middle of the desert in Western Australia and locked us into a detention center like criminals. The ugly brown buildings are surrounded by barbed-wire fences and filled with hundreds of other refugees. After photographing us with a number plate, they give us ID numbers. They won't say our names.

Why are the guards laughing at me? I don't understand when they speak English. They throw a dictionary at me. I don't mind. I copy words from the big book trying to learn this new strange language. I've never held a pen or paper in my hands before.

Two hundred kids. One TV. For hours a day, we crowd into the TV room, fighting over the channel and pulling each other's hair. If it gets too loud, the guards come in and punish us. Sometimes they say troublemakers can't leave their room for a week. Or they might be banned from the TV room for a month. We like to watch a reality show called "Big Brother." Just like us, the contestants live together completely isolated from the outside world. They fight and go crazy on the show. For them, it is just a game. For us, it is so much worse. I am afraid of being sent back to Afghanistan. I worry about my family members left back home. I want to know what is outside these fences."

IMMIGRANT DETENTION CENTER: IMPRISONS PEOPLE WHO DO NOT HAVE LEGAL VISAS GIVING THEM PERMISSION TO BE IN THE COUNTRY, INCLUDING REFUGEES SEEKING ASYLUM

NAJEEBA'S JOURNEY

3 DAYS
from Afghanistan to Pakistan

25 DAYS
hiding in Pakistan

10 DAYS
hiding in Jakarta, Indonesia

10 DAYS
trapped on a boat on the Pacific Ocean

45 DAYS
locked in the Curtin Immigration Detention Centre in Australia

WHAT HAPPENED TO NAJEEBA?

After six weeks in the detention center, Najeeba and her family were sent to Tasmania. After a couple of months, they moved to Western Sydney, where they lived for three years before finally getting permission to stay in Australia. It was difficult for Najeeba to adjust to her new life. She'd never seen a shopping center or a bank machine before. She'd never seen people from other cultures. Even sitting beside a boy at school was frightening.

Today, Najeeba has graduated with a bachelor of medical science and is studying to become an international lawyer. She is a full-time case manager for and the president of Hazara Women of Australia, advocating for the rights of women and refugees, and for the release of children from detention centers.

A year after Najeeba and her family left the Curtin Immigration Detention Centre, it was shut down because it was overcrowded and lacked activities and schooling for children.

Since 2013, Australia has not allowed boat refugees into the country. Children and adult refugees who arrive by boat are sent to detention camps on the remote islands of Nauru or Manus Island, Papua New Guinea, where they are imprisoned indefinitely. Australia's treatment of asylum seekers has been found to violate the United Nations Convention Against Torture. The Australian parliament has launched an investigation but the detention camps remain open.

Hazaras in Afghanistan continue to be persecuted and killed in by ISIS, the Taliban, and other groups.

AFGHANISTAN: A RECENT HISTORY

1999

Taliban attacks force 150,000 Afghans to flee their homes

2000

New Taliban campaign forces tens of thousands of Afghans out of the country
Worst drought in 30 years hits Afghanistan
3.6 million Afghans are refugees, the largest population of refugees in the world

2001

1 million Afghans face famine conditions
American-led invasion of Afghanistan in response to the September 11 attacks in the United States

"We came to Australia because our lives were at RISK. We didn't come here for the tall buildings. We didn't come for the LUXURY. We came for the PEACE. I wouldn't have a LIFE if we stayed. I would have been DEAD at the age of TWELVE."

NoThiNG LeFT To LoSe

Mohamed

13 YEARS OLD
MAPLE, IVORY COAST
2006

66 I thought I was going to spend my whole life in my village with my parents. But this is my life and I cannot fight my destiny. 99

Mohamed handed the smuggler

all his money. He understood crossing the Mediterranean Sea was dangerous. People he knew had died trying. But Mohamed wasn't afraid; he had to get to Italy. There was nothing left for the seventeen-year-old in Libya.

The last time Mohamed was truly afraid was the day his parents died; they were killed by a bomb when he was thirteen. A civil war had been raging in his country, Ivory Coast, for years. Shortly after the bombing, rebels captured Mohamed's village, Maple, and his sixteen-year-old brother Momadi fled. Mohamed was alone. After struggling for months, he decided to leave Ivory Coast to find a place where he could live in peace. He walked to a refugee camp in Guinea, a neighboring country. There, while working at the bus terminal, Mohamed met some human traffickers. He saved up to pay them for passage to Libya, which was also in the middle of a civil war—the unrest would make it easier to smuggle him through. Millions of refugees like Mohamed were fleeing war and poverty in West Africa, North Africa, and the Middle East. They were trying to get to the coast of Libya, where they could cross the Mediterranean Sea and seek asylum in Europe.

Now, after a long journey filled with suffering, Mohamed was boarding a boat for Europe. All he had were the clothes on his back. But he didn't care. Mohamed was desperate to leave Libya. He and other refugees were treated very cruelly there—imprisoned, mistreated by employers, and attacked and robbed by gangs. Maybe life in Italy would be better.

The civil war in Ivory Coast started in 2002 when renegade soldiers tried to oust the president. Muslim rebels in the north were fighting the government-controlled Christian faction in the south. In 2007, the two sides signed an agreement to end the conflict, but the violence continues.

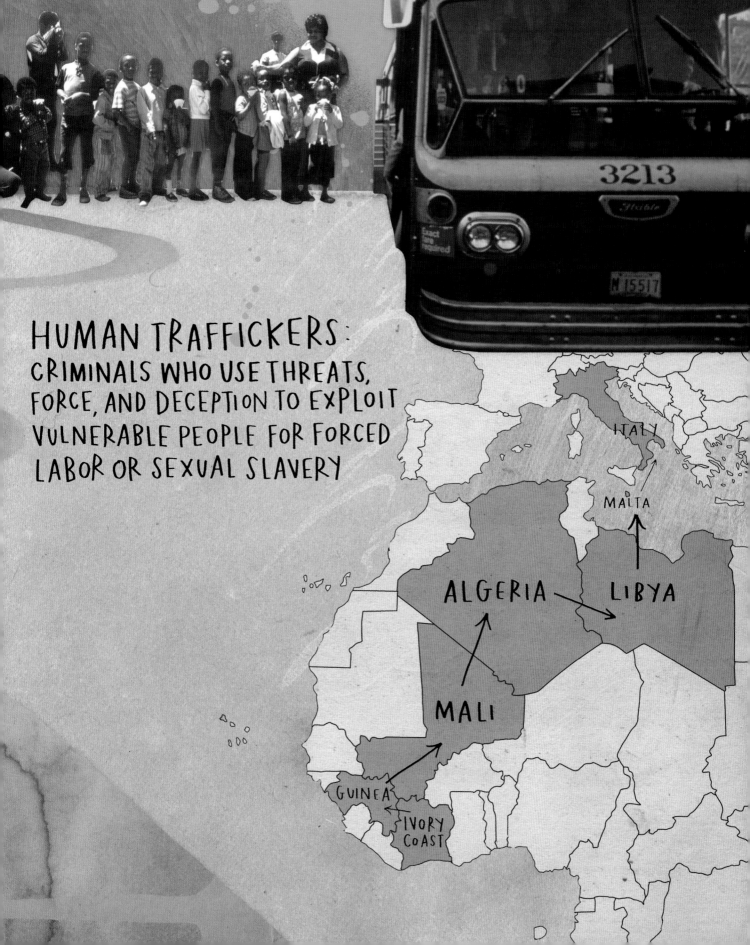

HUMAN TRAFFICKERS:
CRIMINALS WHO USE THREATS, FORCE, AND DECEPTION TO EXPLOIT VULNERABLE PEOPLE FOR FORCED LABOR OR SEXUAL SLAVERY

3213

N 15517

ITALY

MALTA

ALGERIA

LIBYA

MALI

GUINEA

IVORY COAST

"The narrow, open wooden boat is much too small for all thirty-two of us, but the smugglers push us on anyway. One steers us away from the coast but, once we're far from shore, he gets into another boat and goes back to Libya. In exchange for free passage, two of the passengers are left to pilot the boat. They yell and fight, arguing over which way to go.

Up and down, the boat rocks on the choppy Mediterranean. I sit at the very front and hold on tight. I don't know how to swim. There are no life jackets or bailing cans. People are crying and talking nervously. We're in danger of drowning but I don't care. I have nothing to lose.

For three days, we drift at sea. We sit drenched from the spray of the seawater. We're hungry. The traffickers didn't let us bring any food or water on the boat because it would take up too much room. Once a day we eat the biscuits they left us. I fall asleep. I dream I am with friends from Ivory Coast, happy and safe."

"We're in DANGER of DROWNING but I don't care."

At last, we see land! We've made it to Malta, an island in the Mediterranean. I help people out of the boat onto the beach. Some can't walk—the seawater shrank their pants and cut off the circulation in their legs. The authorities take us to a migrant camp, locking us into old army barracks, crowded with other refugees. They treat us like prisoners. All I do is sleep and eat. No activities, no school. All day long I just wait to get out.

After one year, I moved to a new migrant center. It is better. They let us out to go to work. I help a man whitewash houses and do odd jobs. I find a smuggler with a tourist boat who will take me to Italy. The trip takes less than a day but I must pay him $1,200. Will I ever get there?

"They treat us like PRISONERS."

When immigrants arrive in Europe, they are detained in overcrowded migrant camps. Although many are refugees who have the right to asylum under international law because they have been forced out of their home country, they live under the same conditions as migrants who enter the country illegally.

MOHAMED'S JOURNEY

2006
Leaves Ivory Coast

2007
Works in Guinea, Mali, and Algeria to pay human traffickers for transport

2008
Arrives in Libya; arrested and imprisoned for five months

2009
Crosses the Mediterranean Sea to Malta; imprisoned in migrant camp

2010
Arrives in Italy

"A lot of people DON'T UNDERSTAND what it means to SUFFER HARDSHIP because they've never experienced it. When you MIGRATE, it's a SCHOOL OF LIFE."

WHAT HAPPENED TO MOHAMED?

After six months, Mohamed saved up enough money to pay for passage from Malta to Sicily. The smuggler abandoned him once they reached the shore—Mohamed had no idea where he was or where he should go. Luckily, a Tunisian man stopped and asked if he needed help. The man and some of his friends bought Mohamed a ticket to Rome, where he slept outside the Termini train station with other homeless people. All he had was a plastic bag full of his belongings and a piece of cardboard to sleep on. After a few months, Mohamed moved to a center for unaccompanied minor migrants called Civico Zero. There he studied Italian, got training to work in a hotel, and learned photography. Mohamed now works as a hotel porter and spends his free time taking photos. He has had photography shows throughout Italy, including one at the parliamentary library. Mohamed and his brother, Momadi, who lives in Mali, have been reunited.

Each year, a million refugees fleeing war, conflict, and persecution risk their lives crossing the Mediterranean. Tens of thousands of them are unaccompanied migrants like Mohamed, children traveling alone without any adult. Even if they survive the dangerous crossing, life in Europe is not easy. Refugees face a great deal of discrimination, and struggle to find a place to live and go to school, a job, and adequate health care.

WHERE ARE THE BOAT REFUGEES COMING FROM?

1. Syria
2. Afghanistan
3. Eritrea
4. Somalia
5. Nigeria

Source: The UN Refugee Agency, June 29, 2015

THEY CAME BY BOAT:
FROM WWII TO TODAY

1939

German Jews on the SS *St. Louis* escaping anti-Semitic Nazi policies are refused entry into Cuba and forced to return to Europe

1942

Hong Kong refugees escape and flee to Canada after the British colony is surrendered to Japan during World War II

1948

Millions of eastern Europeans displaced by World War II find new homes in North America

1975

Hundreds of thousands of refugees from Vietnam, Cambodia, and Laos—known as the "boat people"—risk their lives on the South China Sea to escape attacks and war

1980

In the Mariel Boatlift, 125,000 Cubans immigrate to Florida as political refugees, escaping the Cuban government's Communist policies

Haitians fleeing a brutal dictatorship are granted refugee status in the United States, after being denied entry for a decade

1987

Tamils from Sri Lanka and Sikhs from India land in Nova Scotia, Canada, seeking refuge from the discrimination they face in their countries

1994

Cubans seeking political asylum in the United States board small boats and rafts but are denied entry

1999

Chinese boat migrants who face political persecution seek asylum in Vancouver, Canada

2000

Afghans and Iraqis escape wars in their homelands and secure passage to Australia

2001

Afghan asylum seekers rescued by the cargo ship *Tampa* are refused entry into Australia

2010

Tamil refugees from Sri Lanka face prejudice and delays when they seek asylum in Canada

2012

Civil war in Syria causes persecuted and displaced citizens to cross the Mediterranean Sea seeking refuge

Civil war in Libya makes it easier to transport West African, North African, and Middle Eastern refugees seeking asylum in Europe across the Mediterranean Sea

2014

Rohingya Muslims, denied citizenship and persecuted in Myanmar, cross the Bay of Bengal for a new life in Indonesia or Malaysia

2015

Syrian refugees fleeing war and terrorism cross the Aegean Sea to Greece

Somali and Ethiopian refugees desperate to escape conflict and poverty in their countries risk their lives to sail to conflict-ridden Yemen

More than 1 million refugees from Syria, Afghanistan, Iraq, and other countries cross the Mediterranean Sea seeking refugee in Europe; an average of two refugee children drown each day in the Mediterranean on their way to Europe

2016

An estimated 2,000 people per day risk their lives crossing the Mediterranean Sea

RESOURCES

Amnesty International, www.amnesty.org/en

Médecins Sans Frontières, www.msf.org

The Migrants' Files, www.themigrantsfiles.com

Refuge Denied: The St. Louis *Passengers and the Holocaust.* Sarah A. Ogilvie and Scott Miller. Madison, Wis.: University of Wisconsin Press, 2006.

Simon Fraser University Digitized Collections, Vietnamese Boat People Collection, http://digital.lib.sfu.ca/vietnamese-collection

UNICEF, www.unicef.org

United Nations Educational, Scientific and Cultural Organization, unesco.org

The United Nations Refugee Agency, www.unhcr.org

United States Holocaust Memorial Museum, www.ushmm.org

Vietnamese American Oral History Project, University of California, Irvine, sites.uci.edu/vaohp/

Voices of Mariel Documentary. Directed by James Carleton. Story Concept by Dr. José Garcia, InFocus Pictures, 2011.

Acknowledgments

When Annick Press approached me to do a book about boat refugees, I was immediately drawn to the project. I was feeling overwhelmed by the news reports of refugees crossing the Mediterranean Sea and was eager to take action in the way that I know best—making sense of issues for myself by making sense of it for young people.

I'm extremely grateful to Phu, José, Najeeba, and Mohamed for sharing their moving stories and for all that they've taught me. And I'm indebted to the individuals and organizations who connected me with them—The University of California's Vietnamese American Oral History Project, Amnesty International Australia, Hazara Women of Australia, and Save the Children Italia. I'm especially thankful for Rome-based journalist Megan Williams responding to my plaintive e-mail and for generously interviewing Mohamed, translating his story, and patiently fielding my numerous follow-up queries. Thank you to the United States Holocaust Memorial Museum for preserving Ruth's oral history and allowing me to use it. Sincere thanks to photographers Lucas Allen and Flavio Scollo, whose beautiful portraits appear in the book. A special thank you to Krisztina Andre, Geo Mesmer, and the German Alliance for Civilian Assistance who, despite the crisis they faced on the Balkan migrant route, made time to look for young Syrian refugees who were able to share their stories.

The research and reporting of UNHRC, UNESCO, Amnesty International, UNICEF, and Médicins Sans Frontières were invaluable in the development of this book. The work of countless journalists and news agencies was also crucial to deepening my understanding of refugee crises past and present, in particular, the Canadian and Australian Broadcasting Corporations, *The New York Times*, *The Economist*, BBC News, NPR, *Miami Herald*, and *New Internationalist*.

Huge thanks to the Annick Press team for their support of this project. Special thanks to Katie Hearn for seeing what this book could be and guiding me so incisively and amiably to get there. I'm immensely grateful to Eleanor Shakespeare for sharing her extraordinary talents: her beautiful artwork has brought to the page what was whirling in my heart.

CREDITS

Front cover: cropped photograph of crowded boat transporting African refugees, © iStock. com/Guenter Guni; map used throughout, © Michello/Dreamstime.com; page i: people in boat, © iStock.com/helenecanada; pages ii, iii: life buoy, © Claudiodivizia/Dreamstime. com; Turned Away: pages 1, 4: detail of photograph of Eva Schravel and Ruth Zellner, Yad Vashem Photo Archive, courtesy of Dr. Herbert Fiedler; page 2: detail of immigration identification card issued by the Cuban government to St. Louis passenger, © United States Holocaust Memorial Museum, courtesy of Faye Flamberg Ben-Saull; page 3: cropped photograph of St. Louis, © Sueddeutsche Zeitung Photo/Alamy Stock Photo; detail of telegram sent by the passengers of the MS St. Louis, © United States Holocaust Memorial Museum, courtesy Betty Troper Yaeger; Ruth's story developed based on United States Holocaust Memorial Museum Record Group 50.030*0402, Oral History, Interview with Ruth Zellner, RG 50.030.0402_trs_en.pdf.; Fighting to Survive: pages 11, 19: photos of Phu courtesy of Phu Do Nguyen; pages 12, 13: detail of photographs of left and right tank, Department of Defense, Department of the Navy, U.S. Marine Corps: series: Black and White Photographs of Marine Corps Activities in Vietnam, 1962–1975: courtesy NARA: 127-GVB-335-A374178 and 127-GVB-334-A372201; figure climbing ladder, © iStock.com/andresrimaging; page 17: Vietnamese refugees in boat, Department of Defense, American Forces Information Service, Defense Visual Information Center, 1994, series: Combined Military Service Digital Photographic Files, 1982–2007: courtesy NARA: 330-CFD-DN-SN-84-09733; Newspaper quote from Editorial, *The Wichita Eagle*, March 6, 1978; Stormy Seas: pages 21, 23: photos of José and family courtesy of Dr. José Garcia; pages 24, 25: fishing boats, © iStock.com/Yails and © iStock.com/terex; Fidel Castro, Keystone Pictures USA/Alamy Stock Photo; Jimmy Carter, Marion S. Trikosko, photographer: Library of Congress Prints and Photographs Division, LC-U9-39080B-11A; Fidel Castro quote taken from "Our Criminals are Leaving to their Allies in the US", May Day Address, May 1, 1980, Jose Marti Revolution Square; Jimmy Carter quote taken from The American Presidency Project. President Jimmy Carter, Question and Answer Session at the League of Women Voters Biennal National Convention, May 5, 1980. http://www.presidency.ucsb.edu/ws/?pid=33365; pages 26, 27: shrimp boat, © iStock.com/Nicolas McComber; Fenced In: page 30: Afghan National Air Corp L-39 Albatross jets, photo by Master Sgt. Cecilio Ricardo; barbed wire, © iStock.com/hanibaram; Afghan houses, © iStock.com/Mie Ahmt; page 31; photo of Najeeba © Lucas Allen; pages 34, 35: people in boat, © iStock.com/helenecanada; pages 36, 37: patched boat bottom, © iStock.com/RanieriMeloni; page 39: flipped detail of photograph of refugees waiting in line, © Anjo Kan/Dreamstime.com; page 41: clapping hands, © iStock.com/RapidEye; Nothing Left to Lose: pages 42, 43: African rooftops, © iStock.com/Peeter Viisimaa; photo of Mohamed on page 43 Courtesy of Flavio Scollo; pages 46, 47: flipped cropped photograph of crowded boat transporting African refugees, © iStock.com/Guenter Guni; pages 48, 49: legs, © iStock.com/RanieriMeloni and © iStock.com/UygarGeographic; pages 50, 51: coins, © iStock.com/MARIA TOUTOUDAKI; key, © June M Sobrito/Dreamstime.com; camera, © iStock.com/pakornkrit; overlaid photos at the top of page 50 Courtesy of Mohamed Keita, www.mohamedkeita.it; endpapers: planks, © stockcreations/Dreamstime.com